DREAMLAND

SUPER PICTURE DICTIONARY

Compiled by:
Lata & Priyanka

DREAMLAND PUBLICATIONS

J-128, KIRTI NAGAR, NEW DELHI - 110 015, INDIA
Tel : +91-11-2510 6050, 2543 5657
E-mail: dreamland@dreamlandpublications.com
Shop online at www.dreamlandpublications.com
Follow us on www.instagram.com/dreamland.publications

Published in 2023 by
DREAMLAND PUBLICATIONS
J-128, Kirti Nagar, New Delhi - 110 015, India
Tel : +91-11-2510 6050, 2543 5657
Copyright © 2023 Dreamland Publications

ISBN 978-93-5089-334-0

Printed in India

PREFACE

Super Picture Dictionary has been designed for the children of seven years and up. This dictionary not only contains words with simple and easy-to-understand meanings, but also exciting colourful images. These images will make it easy for children to learn the meanings of words and build their language skills. We hope this dictionary will help children enrich their vocabulary and make them understand the words on hearing them.

—Publisher

INTRODUCTION

The Super Picture Dictionary with colourful images to help children learn new words and their meaning easily.

Words are fun. We use them every day.

Aeroplane   **Baby**

We read words and use them to talk.

Card   **Attend**

She sent an invitation card for her birthday party.

We attend school five days a week.

We use words to write.

Pencil

A group of words arranged systematically form a sentence. A sentence shows how words are used in practice.

Pen

This is a fountain pen.

HERE IS YOUR DICTIONARY

This dictionary is filled with more than 1000 words. Each word is accompanied by an image. Many words are the kind that you use everyday. Some new words have been introduced to enrich your vocabulary. Each word has been explained clearly and has its meaning in its definition.

Alphabetical order
All the words in dictionary are arranged in alphabetical order. This means that all words that begin with 'A' are grouped together, and so on.

Bubble a ball of air or gas in liquid. The children like to blow bubbles into water through a straw.

Bucket an open container with a handle, used for carrying and holding things, especially water.

Buckle a flat pin within a frame, used for joining the ends of a belt.

Bud a young flower leaf. The bush has plenty of buds.

Buffalo a large wild animal like a cow with a large head and thick hair on its shoulder and neck.

Building a structure that has roof and walls, like a house, or school. There is a new building being put up near the shopping centre.

Bulldozer a large tractor with a blade at the front. A bulldozer is used to move earth and rocks.

Bun a small round flat bread roll. I had fresh baked bun with a cup of coffee.

Bunch a number of things of the same type which are growing or fastened together: a bunch of bananas / grapes, etc

Burger a kind of sandwich consisting of a bun, a cooked patty, and often other ingredients such as cheese, onion slices, lettuce, etc.

20

Images
The images accompanying the words will help you to understand the meaning of a word.

Example sentences
These sentences show how the word can be used.

3

Super Picture Dictionary contains a variety of words in alphabetical order with colourful images that bring words to life and make learning fun.

A is the first letter of the English Alphabet.

Able

to have the skill to do something means one can do it. He is able to play guitar very well.

About

nearly, reasonably close to. Julie told Marry about the new story she read.

Above

over or in a higher place. An aeroplane is flying in the sky above our heads.

Absorb

to take in a liquid. A sponge absorbs water.

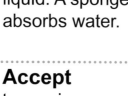

Accept

to receive or take something willingly that is offered.

Accident

something that happens by chance. The accident happened at 4 p.m.

Accordion

a portable musical instrument with reeds blown by bellows and played by means of keys and buttons.

Ace

(a) the highest playing card.
(b) a person who is very good at something.

Ache

to feel a continuous dull pain. My tooth is aching very badly.

Acorn

a seed or fruit of the oak tree. Tom likes to eat acorns.

Acrobat

a person who does clever balancing tricks in a circus or on the stage.

Across

from one side to the other. The new bridge makes it easy to get across.

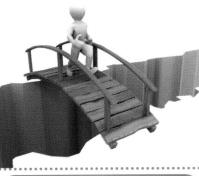

Act

to perform in a play or film. All of them acted very well in the play.

Actor

a person who performs in a play, movie, etc. We see actors on television, in films and in plays.

Add

to put numbers together to find the total. Add 2 and 2 to get 4.

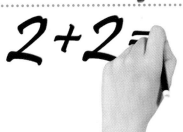

$$2 + 2 =$$

Address

details of where someone lives or works and where letters, parcels, etc. can be sent.

Admire

to have high regard for someone. John admires his teacher very much.

Adult

a grown-up man or woman. Adults are more experienced than children.

Aerobics

a system of exercises to improve the body's ability. Aerobics is usually done along with music.

Aeroplane

a large flying machine with wings and an engine, used for carrying passengers and goods.

Afraid

scared; when someone is afraid, they feel fear.

After

following something; later in time or place. Tony is after the ball.

Afternoon

the part of the day between midday and evening.

Again

to do something once more. Don't play the same tune again.

Age

the number of years someone has lived.

Ahead

in the front. He is ahead of his friends.

Aim

to have a purpose, or goal. Bob's aim was to reach on the top.

Air

air is the mixture of gases that surround the earth. We breathe air in and out.

Airport

a place where aeroplanes land and take off from. Tom went to the airport to receive his father.

Alarm-clock

clock that you can set to ring a bell at a particular time and wake you up. I set the alarm-clock for 5 o'clock.

Album

a book with blank pages for collecting things like stamps or photographs.

Alike

like one another. Harry and his brother look alike.

Alive

living, not dead. The pigeon is alive.

All

the whole of, or everything. There is furniture for all rooms.

Alligator

an animal with a long tail and big teeth that lives around river and lakes.

Allow

permit, to let something happen.

Almond

an oval nut that is good to eat. Almonds can be eaten raw, roasted, or salted.

Almost

very nearly but not completely. Megan is almost through with her work.

Alone

without any other people or without the company of others. Sam is alone in his room.

Alphabet

the letters used in writing a language. There are 26 alphabets in English language.

Always

at all times. The sun always rises in the east.

Ambulance

a vehicle for taking people, who are ill or hurt to and from the hospital.

Anchor

a heavy hook that is dropped to the bottom of the sea to stop a ship from floating away. The ship dropped the anchor.

Angry

a feeling of annoyance; when someone is angry they may want to speak loudly or fight.

Animal

a living thing that can move about by itself; an animal kingdom.

Ankle
part of the body between the leg and the foot that bends.

Another
some other, one more. We have got another apple.

Answer
something you say or write after a question. To answer the question, Tony raised his hand.

Ant
an insect that lives in groups. An ant has six legs.

Antler
a type of hard horn on the head of a deer.

Ape
a large animal that has no tail and is related to the monkeys. There were two apes in the zoo.

Apple
a delicious fruit that grows on trees. Apples may be red, yellow, or green.

Apricot
a round fruit with yellow or orange skin and a large seed inside.

Apron
a piece of cloth that you put on top of your clothes to keep them clean usually while cooking.

Aquarium
a plastic or glass box filled with water for keeping fish in.

Archer
a person who shoots with bow and arrow.

Area
part of a place or town, etc.

Argue
to strongly disagree. The children are arguing over a TV programme.

Arm

part of your body between your shoulder and hand.

Armour

a metal suit worn for protection in a battle. In olden times, knights wore suits of armour during battle.

Army

an organised group of soldiers who are trained to fight on land.

Arrange

to put in order; to make something neat. The blocks have been arranged in alphabetical order.

Arrive

to come to a place, or reach some place. They arrived late as their flight was delayed.

Arrow

a thin stick with a sharp point at one end, which is shot from a bow.

Artificial

not real, created by people; artificial flowers.

Artist

a person who makes art. He draws and paints, he is a very good artist.

Asleep

sleeping. He was so tired that he fell asleep on his books.

Ask

to say something in order to get an answer or some information. The teacher asked Harry to spell his name.

Assembly

a group of people gathered together, meeting.

Astronaut

a person who travels in a spacecraft to reach outerspace. An astronaut wears a special set of clothing.

Athlete

someone who trains to be good at running, jumping or throwing. John and Jacob are good athletes.

Atlas

a book that contains maps and geographical information. I used an atlas to find my way around the city.

Attack

to be violent, to try to hurt someone. Martin attacked Sam with a hammer.

Attend

to be present at. We attend school five days a week.

Attention

the act of listening to or looking at something carefully.

Author

a person who writes stories, books, or any other written work. She is a good author.

Autograph

a signature, especially that of a celebrity. May I have your autograph?

Autumn

the time of year between the summer and the winter.

Awake

not sleeping, to wake up. James awoke early in the morning.

Award

something given as a prize for something that somebody has done.

Axe

a tool with a handle and a sharp piece of metal at the end that is used for chopping wood or cutting down trees.

a b c d e f g h i j k l m n o p q r s t u v w x y z

Bb

B is the second letter of the English Alphabet.

Baboon
a kind of large monkey with a dog-like face. Baboons live in Africa and South Asia.

Baby
a very young child who has not yet begun to walk, or talk.

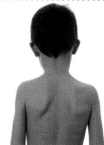

Back
the rear surface of the human body from the shoulders to the hips. Put some oil on my back.

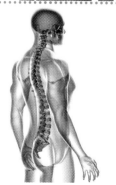

Backbone
the row of connected bones that go down the middle of your back. Backbone is also called a spine.

Background
the scenes which designs, or patterns are viewed, or represented. A photograph with flowers in the background.

Backpack
a type of bag that is carried on one's back. I always carry my books in my backpack.

Bad
not good, or pleasant. Rocky is a bad boy, stay away from him.

Badge
a piece of plastic, metal, or cloth that one puts on one's clothes to signify a mark of office, membership, achievement, etc.

EXECUTIVE
BODYGUARD

Badminton
a sport played with racket and shuttlecock.

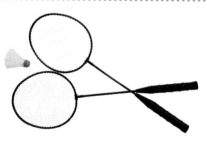

Bag
a container made from cloth, plastic, leather, etc., usually with one, or two handles, used to carry things in. He kept all the books in his bag.

Ball

an object that you throw, hit, or kick in games. Some games are played with a ball.

Ballet

an art form using dancing, music, scenery to convey a story, or a theme. She wants to be a ballet dancer.

Balloon

a brightly coloured rubber, inflated with gas, or with air gas and used for children's decoration, or as playing. We decorated the house with balloons for party.

Banana

a long curved fruit, having a thick yellow skin which usually has a soft, sweet, whitish pulp. I like bananas for breakfast.

Band

a small group of musicians who play popular music together, often with a singer, or singers. He is a singer with a band.

Bandage

a strip of a fabric used to cover up the wound. I wrapped a bandage around my ankle to give it some support.

Barn

a large farm building for keeping livestock, or storing crops, or hay.

Basket

a container made of thin strips for holding, or carrying things. There are fresh vegetables in the basket.

Bat

(a) a piece of wood for hitting a ball in a game. (b) a small mammal that usually flies at night.

Bath

wash (someone) while immersing him or her in a container of water: It's your turn to bath the baby.

Battery

a device that is placed inside a clock, radio, toy, etc. and that produces the power that makes it work.

Beach

the sandy part beside the sea. I love going to the beach in the summer time.

Beads

a small piece of material pierced for threading on a string.
A string of beads.

Beak

the hard curved, or pointed part of the bird's mouth. The parrot has a curved beak.

Bean

a seed of various plants that is cooked and eaten. I like baked beans on toast.

Bear

a large heavy animal that has long shaggy hair. There are many kinds of bear: a black bear, grizzly bear.

Beard

the hair that grows around a man's chin and cheeks.

Beautiful

very pleasant. You have the most beautiful smile and really look very pretty.

Beaver

a small animal that has wide flat tail and thick fur.

Bed

a piece of furniture for sleeping on.
I am tired, I am going to bed.

Bee

a flying insect that has yellow and black bands and can sting you.

Beehive

a structure in which you keep bees and from which you collect their honey.

Beetle

an insect with a smooth hard back.

Before

earlier than a particular time. She was fairly fat before she started regular exercises.

Begin

to start. Please begin the race now. Get, set and go!

Bell

a hollow metal object, often shaped like a cup, that makes a ringing sound when hit by a small piece of metal inside it. The children left the classroom when the bell rang.

Belong

to be in the right, or suitable place. This box belongs to the person living next door.

Belt

a narrow piece of leather , or cloth that you wear around your waist to keep your clothes in place.

Bench

a hard seat made of wood or metal. The bench is lying in a garden.

Bend

to stoop. She bent over to touch her foot.

Beneath

under something. She hid herself down beneath the table.

Berry

a small round juicy fruit without a stone. Raspberry, strawberry, and blackberry are all berries.

Beside

next to something. She stood beside him during party.

Beverage

any liquid besides water that is fit for drinking.

Beware

warning somebody to be careful. Beware of the dog!

Bicycle

a vehicle with two wheels that you ride by pushing pedals with your feet.

Bike

a bicycle or a motorcycle. I brought a brand new red colour bike.

Bingo

a game in which players match numbers on a card with number drawn at random.

Binocular

a pair of lenses placed together through which you can see far off things more clearly.

Bird

an animal that has wings, feathers and lays eggs. The macaw is a bird of parrot family, with bright feathers and a long tail..

Birthday

the day of the year on which a person is born. I am baking birthday cake for Alex.

Bite

to cut into something with your teeth. He had a big bite of a piece of pizza.

Black

the darkest of all colours. This hat is black.

Blackberry

a sweet, dark purple berry that grows on a thorny bush.

Blackboard

a hard smooth usually dark surface used especially in a classroom for writing, or drawing on with chalk.

Blanket

a large cover, often made of wool, used especially on beds to keep people warm. It's going to get cold tonight, you may need extra blanket.

Blind

unable to see. A band around his eyes blinded him.

Block

a large piece of a solid material that is usually square in shape and has flat sides.

Blood

the red fluid flowing through the bodies of humans and animals. The colour of blood is red.

Blossom

a flower, especially the flower of a fruit tree blossom or bush.

Blow

to push air out of your mouth. Jenny can blow up the balloon.

Blue

having the colour of a clear sky, or the sea. The sky was gloriously blue.

Bluebird

a group of medium-sized birds of the thrush family that lives in North America.

Boat

a small vehicle that people use for travelling on water.

Body

the whole physical structure of a person, or animal, including the head, arms and legs.

Boil

to heat a liquid to the temperature at which it bubbles and turns to steam.

Bolt

a sliding metal bar for fastening a window, or door. Bolt the door.

Bone

any of the hard parts that form the skeleton of the body of a human, or an animal. We all are made of flesh and bones.

a b c d e f g h i j k l m n o p q r s t u v w x y z

b

Book

printed pages that are fastened inside a cover. This is an old book.

Boot

an outer covering for the foot, reaching above the ankle. Sammy bought a new pair of boots.

Bottle

a container usually with a narrow neck made of glass or plastic used for holding liquid.

Bottom

(a) the lowest part of anything.
(b) the part of the body one sits on.

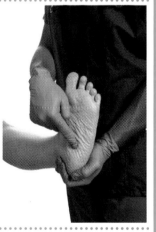

Bow

a knot of cloth or string with two loose ends that is used for decoration on clothes, in hair, etc.

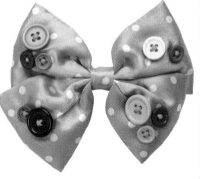

Bowl

a deep round dish. I always eat a bowl of fruit for breakfast.

Box

a container for putting things. Keep all the toys in the box.

Boy

a male child or a young male person. The boy is waiting for his parents to come home.

Bracelet

a piece of jewellery that you wear around the wrist. A gold bracelet.

Brain

an organ inside your head that allows you to think and feel, and controls your body.

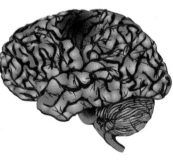

Bread

a type of baked food. A bakery has a good selection of breads and pastries.

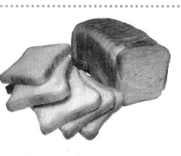

Break

to smash into pieces. Someone broke my pencil.

Breakfast

the first meal that you have in the morning. Never skip your breakfast.

Brick

a rectangular block of baked or sun-dried clay, used in building. The building wall is built of bricks.

Bride

a woman who is getting married, or who has recently married.

Bridge

a structure built over a road, railway line, usually to provide a crossing from one side to the other.

Briefcase

a rectangular case with a handle, often leather, used fo carrying books and papers.

Bright

shining with a lot of light. The room has been decorated in bright colours.

Brooch

a piece of ornament with a pin on the back that you fasten to your clothes.

Brother

a boy, or man who has same parents as you have. My brother Charlie is younger to me.

Brush

an object made of short stiff hairs or wires set in a block of wood or plastic, used for cleaning, painting, and arranging your hair.

a b c d e f g h i j k l m n o p q r s t u v w x y z

Bubble

a ball of air or gas in liquid. The children like to blow bubbles into water through a straw.

Bucket

an open container with a handle, used for carrying and holding things, especially water.

Buckle

a flat pin within a frame, used for joining the ends of a belt.

Bud

a young flower leaf. The bush has plenty of buds.

Buffalo

a large wild animal like a cow with a large head and thick hair on its shoulder and neck.

Building

a structure that has roof and walls, like a house, or school. There is a new building being put up near the shopping centre.

Bulldozer

a large tractor with a blade at the front. A bulldozer is used to move earth and rocks.

Bun

a small round flat bread roll. I had fresh baked bun with a cup of coffee.

Bunch

a number of things of the same type which are growing or fastened together: a bunch of bananas, grapes, etc.

Burger

a kind of sandwich consisting of a bun, a cooked patty, and often other ingredients such as cheese, onion slices, lettuce, etc.

Burn

to produce flames and heat. The flames seemed to burn even brighter.

Bus

a large motor vehicle carrying passengers by road, esp. one serving the public on a fixed route and for a fare.

Butcher

someone who prepares and cuts up meat to be sold.

Butter

a yellow food made from cream that is used as a spread or in cooking.

Butterfly

flying insect with beautiful, large and colourful wings.

Butterscotch

a flavour made from brown sugar and butter used for pouring on ice cream, etc. I love butterscotch ice cream.

Button

a small round flat object on your shirt, coat, etc. Her new coat has five big buttons down the front.

Buy

to get something by paying for it. He spent his pocket-money to buy fruit and vegetables.

Bye

to say goodbye especially when speaking to children, friends or members of your family. Bye everyone! See you later.

a b c d e f g h i j k l m n o p q r s t u v w x y z

C is the third letter of the English Alphabet.

Cactus
a plant with a thick fleshy stem and sharp spines. Cactuses are found in deserts.

Cage
a structure of bars for keeping birds and animals.

Cake
a sweet food made from the mixture of flour, eggs, sugar, and other ingredients, baked and often decorated.

Calculator
a small device that performs mathematical calculations.

Calendar
a table showing days, weeks and months in at least one specific year.

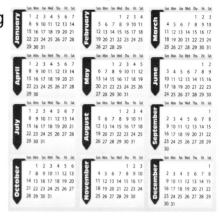

Calf
(a) a young cow or bull.
(b) the back part of one's leg.

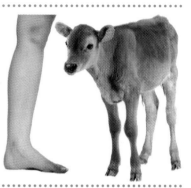

Camel
an animal either with one or two humps on its back, used for carrying people or goods. Camel is a large desert animal.

Camera
a device for taking photographs.

Can
(a) a metal container. A can of cola. (b) to be able to; to be allowed to.

Candle

a stick of wax with a string in it called a wick that you burn to give light.

Candy

a sweet made from sugar or syrup with flavouring colours. Kids love to have candies.

Canoe

a small narrow boat moved by paddles.

Cap

a kind of hat, often with a peak and usually worn as part of a uniform.

Car

a vehicle moving on wheels. She bought a new car.

Card

a piece of thick folded paper, usually with a picture on the front and writing inside. She sent an invitation card for her birthday party.

Carpet

a soft, thick covering for the floor, made from wool or other materials. The floor was covered with a red carpet.

Carrot

an orange vegetable that grows under the ground and has green leaves on its top. My mother chopped some carrots for soup.

Castle

a fortified building with high walls, towers, and big gates.

Casual

(a) clothes that are comfortable, not formal.
(b) someone or something that is relaxed or unconcerned.

Cat

a small, furry animal often kept as a pet. Cats have short legs and a beautiful furry tail.

a b c d e f g h i j k l m n o p q r s t u v w x y z

23

Catch

to take hold of something when it is moving. Sam jumped and tried to catch the ball.

Caterpillar

the larva of a butterfly or moth.

Cattle

a group of cows often kept on a farm for their meat. The cattle are grazing in the paddock.

Cave

a large hollow in the side of a cliff, hill, or underground. Some caves are very long.

Cello

a musical instrument like a violin which you play.

Centipede

a long creature with a lot of tiny legs.

Cereal

a food made from grain, like wheat, oats, mainly eaten with milk for breakfast. Eat a bowl of cereal before going to school.

Chain

made of metal rings joined together. Chains are used for fastening things.

Chair

a separate seat for one person, usually having a back and four legs. This chair is made of plastic.

Chalk

a soft earthy limestone, used for writing.

Chart

a record or plan showing special information, often with lists and diagrams. I bought an alphabet chart for my daughter.

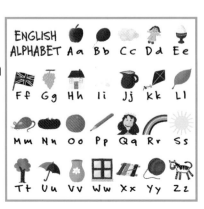

24

Chase

to pursue in order to catch. The police saw a stranger person and chased him.

Cheek

the soft part on each side of your face below your eyes. Sarah kissed her little brother on his cheeks.

Cheese

a solid food made from milk. My mother made delicious cheese sandwich for breakfast.

Cheetah

a wild animal that has yellow coat with black spots and runs very fast.

Chef

the head cook in the restaurant.

Cherry

a small, round, red fruit with a stone. Garnish the cake with cherry in the middle of the creamy top.

Chess

a game for two players played on a black and white board, with sixteen pieces each. Let's play a game of chess.

Chest

the front part of your body between your neck and waist.

Chicken

a kind of a bird that people keep to get eggs or to use as food. Let's have roasted chicken for dinner.

Child

a young human being (boy or girl) below the age of puberty.

Chime

a bell with a musical sound. Wind chime add nice element to my home.

Chimney

a vertical channel that carries smoke away from a fire, furnace, engine, etc.

Chimpanzee

an animal of an ape family, having black or brown fur that lives and hunts in group. We saw lots of chimpanzees at the zoo.

Chin

the part of your face below your mouth. He has a scar on his chin.

Chocolate

a brown-coloured sweet food made from roasted and ground cocoa beans. We all love to eat chocolates.

Chop

to cut in pieces. Mother added finely chopped tomatoes in the hot oil.

Church

a special building where people worship God. Maria goes to the church every Sunday.

Circle

a completely round flat shape. I bought a clock that was round like a circle.

Circus

a travelling show presented by clowns, acrobats, and trained animals in a ring.

City

the large important town. I have a wonderful view of the entire city from my window.

Clap

to hit your hands together loudly. The baby clapped her hands joyfully.

Classroom

a room in a school where you have lessons. The teacher walked into the classroom, greeted the students, and took attendance.

Claw

the hard, sharp, curved nail on the foot of a bird or an animal. The eagle has sharp nails on its claws.

Clean

neat and tidy; free from dirt, smoke, or harmful substances. Children tried to clean the floor.

Clear

easy to see through. The water is clear and fit for drinking.

Climb

to move upwards. He climbed up to save himself with the help of rope.

Clock

an instrument that tells the time. Look at the clock! It's almost eight o'clock! We must hurry.

Clothes

things that you wear, like shirt and trousers. I have some new clothes for my birthday.

Cloud

a visible grey or white mass of very small drops of water that floats in the sky.

Clown

the funny man in a circus who makes people laugh.

Club

an organisation for people who have common interest in a particular activity. My brother has joined a golf club.

Coal

a black substance used as a fuel. Coal is a non-renewable source of energy.

Coat

a piece of warm clothing that is worn over other clothes. A coat has long sleeves and keeps us warm. Billy bought a new winter coat.

Cobweb

a thin, sticky thread, made by a spider to catch flies and insects.

Cockroach

an insect that lives in dark, warm places and comes out at night looking for food.

Coconut

a very large nut with a hard, brown shell and sweet, white flesh. I love to eat coconut flesh.

Coin

a piece of money made of metal. I have a collection of some old coins.

Cold

an infection in which the nose and the throat become inflamed. She caught a cold yesterday.

Colour

colour of something is the special look it has which we call by names like red, blue, pink, etc. Blue is my favourite colour.

Comb

A strip of plastic, metal, or wood with a row of narrow teeth, used for untangling or arranging the hair.

Combo

A combination, typically of different foods: "the combo platter".

28

Compact disc

a small, round, flat piece of plastic, with music or information stored on it.

Compass

an instrument for finding direction, with a needle that always points to the north.

Computer

a machine that stores information and can solve mathematical sums quickly. We are learning how to use computers at school.

Continent

main areas of land in the world. There are seven continents in the world.

Cook

a person who prepares food for eating.
Jane is a very good cook.

Cookie

a small, flat cake, which has been baked until it is hard.
I had a cup of coffee and some cookies.

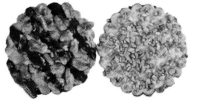

Corn

the long hard part of the maize (corn) plant that the rows of yellow grains grow on.

Corner

a place where two converging sides or edges meet.

Country

a large area of land with its own government. Germany is a beautiful country.

GERMANY

Cow

a female farm animal that produces milk. Cows eat grass. They are kept for their milk.

Crab

a sea animal with eight legs, hard shell and two large claws at the front of its body.

Crayon

a coloured pencil or a stick used for colouring and drawing.
Teacher said to draw a picture and fill the colours using crayons.

Crocodile

a large animal with a long tail, tough skin and big jaws that lives in rivers. Crocodiles have sharp teeth.

Crow

a large black bird that is known for its harsh cry, or caw.

Crowd

a large number of people gathered together. There were crowds of students in the college.

Crown

a covering made of gold and decorated with jewels, worn by kings and queens on their heads.

Cry

to shed tears. The baby was crying for a ball.

Cucumber

a long thin round vegetable with green skin and white flesh. Cucumbers are eaten in salads.

Cuddle

to put your arms around someone in a loving way. We love to cuddle our children.

Cup

a small, round, open container for a drink, usually with a handle. I like to have a coffee in my favourite red cup.

Cupboard

a piece of furniture with doors and sometimes shelves, used for storing clothes, food, plates, etc. Please dry the plates, and put them in the cupboard.

Curd

the soft, white substance that forms when milk turns sour, used as a food or to make cheese.

Currant

a small, sour, red, white, or black berry. Currants are used for making jams and jellies.

Cutlery

knives, forks and spoons that you use for eating food.

Cymbal

a musical instrument in the form of a thin round metal plate, which you play by hitting it with a stick or by hitting two of them together.

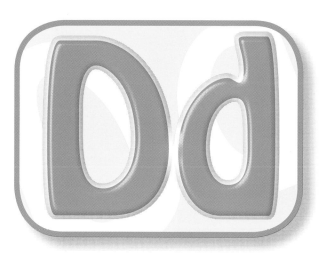

D is the fourth letter of the English Alphabet.

Daffodil
a plant with bright yellow or creamy white flower with a centre shaped like a cup that grows in spring.

Daisy
a small white flower with a yellow centre and lots of white or coloured petals.

Dance
to move your feet and body with music. After the wedding everyone danced until midnight.

Danger
a thing that causes or is likely to cause harm or injury.
He is in danger.

Dark
no light. Soon it will be dark enough to see the stars.

Daughter
a female child. My daughter Myra is very loving and sweet.

Dawn
to begin to grow light as the sun rises. There was a lovely dawn this morning. The sky was red.

Day
the period of light from dawn to dusk. We spent the day in the garden that was full of flowers.

Decorate
to make something look more attractive by putting nice things on it. Decorate the house with colourful ribbons.

Deer

a fast-running wild animal with thin legs.
We saw some deer in the zoo. Deer eats grass and has horns.

Delicious

something that tastes or smells very good.
The jelly looks extremely delicious.

Dentist

someone whose job is to keep your teeth clean and healthy.
She goes to the dentist for a check-up every six months.

Desert

a large area of dry land that gets little or no rain.

Desk

a table, with drawers, used for working at or writing on. Please put the books on my desk.

Dessert

sweet food that you eat at the end of your meal. We had ice cream with honey and chocolate for dessert.

Dew

small drops of water condensed from air, usually at night onto cool surfaces.
The leaf is wet with early morning dew.

Diamond

very hard stone which is clear like glass and is used in jewellery.
My mother has a ring with huge diamond in the middle of it.

Diary

a book in which you write what happens each day.
Kelly kept a diary since she was twelve.

Dice

small cubes with faces bearing 1-6 spots, used in playing games.

Dictionary
a book containing words of a language alphabetically arranged, with their meanings, etc.

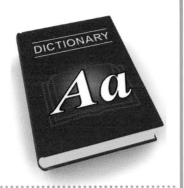

Dirty
not clean; needing to be washed.
Try not to get your clothes dirty.

Different
things which are not like each other.
I wanted something a bit different, so, I bought six neckties.

Doctor
someone who is trained to treat the sick people.
Sammy was treated by his family doctor.

Dig
to turn over the soil with a spade. It is difficult to dig the ground when it is hard.

Dog
an animal with four legs which eats meat and which people keep as a pet. I have white dog called Bruno.

Dinner
the main meal that you eat in the evening or midday. We had curry and rice for dinner last night.

Doll
a children's toy that looks like a person. My sister has plenty of dolls.

Dinosaur
an animal that lived millions of years ago, but now it no longer exists. There were many types of dinosaur.

Dollar
the main unit of money that is used in some countries. She had to pay hundreds of dollars in auto repairs.

a b c **d** e f g h i j k l m n o p q r s t u v w x y z

d

Dolphin

a large sea animal, similar to fish, with a long nose and a curved fin on the back.

Donkey

a long-eared animal, related to horse. People use donkey to carry heavy loads.

Doughnut

a small usually ring-shaped cake fried in fat with sweet coatings.

Door

a large flat object that opens and closes at the entrance of a building, room, etc. Marc came into the room, and opened the door.

Dove

a white bird that makes a gentle, cooing sound. Dove is a sign of peace.

Dozen

a set of twelve things or people. There were a dozen of cherry tomatoes.

Dragon

a large imaginary creature in old stories that has wings and a long pointed tail and breathes out fire.

Draw

to make a picture with a pencil, pen, etc. He began to draw a beautiful picture with a sketch pen.

Drawer

a sliding box in a piece of furniture, used for storing things. The photos are in the top drawer of my desk.

Dream

thoughts and pictures that pass through your mind while you are sleeping. Kate dreamt that she has become a doctor.

Dress

clothes that are suitable for a particular occasion. The children wore different dresses for the party.

Drill

a sharp metal tool that is used to make holes.

Drink

a liquid that you swallow. We must drink eight glasses of water everyday.

Drive

to control a vehicle. How old you have to be to drive a car?

Drop

(a) small particle of a liquid. Dew drops fell on leaves at night. (b) fall or let something fall, usually by accident.

Drum

a hollow musical instrument that makes a deep sound when you hit it. She drummed while he played the guitar.

Duck

a water bird with short legs and flat feet. Look at the ducks swimming across the lake.

Dust

a fine powder that consists of very small pieces of sand, earth, etc.

Duster

a cloth or other soft material for removing dust.

Dwarf

a person who is markedly small, below average size.

a
b
c
d
e
f
g
h
i
j
k
l
m
n
o
p
q
r
s
t
u
v
w
x
y
z

d

E is the fifth letter of the English Alphabet.

Eagle
a large, strong bird with a hooked beak and sharp claws that kills other birds and animals for food.

Ear
the part of the body used for hearing.
We have two ears.

Earth
the planet on which we live.
The earth is big and round.

Eat
to chew and swallow food.
Norman eats banana for breakfast.

Egg
an oval object with a shell that a female bird produces and a baby bird develops in. Eggs laid by hen are used as food.

Elbow
the joints that connects the upper and the lower parts of your arm. Your elbow is where your arm bends.

Electricity
energy or power that we use for lightning and heating, and to make machines work. We must switch off the lights when not in use to save electricity.

Elephant
a very large animal, with a thick, leathery skin, a long trunk, curved tusks and big fan shaped ears.

Empty
containing nothing. The cup is empty. There is nothing in it.

Emu

a swift-running Australian bird that has long legs and cannot fly. An emu looks like an ostrich.

Enjoy

to get pleasure from something. Everyone enjoyed themselves in the party.

Envelope

a folded paper cover that you put a letter in.
Put a stamp on the envelope before you post it.

Eraser

a small piece of rubber used for removing pencil mistakes.

Escape

to get away. Two men escaped from prison yesterday.

Evergreen

a tree or plant that keeps its leaves throughout the year. Most pines are evergreen trees.

Excite

to make someone interested, happy and lively.

Exercise

an activity that you do to make your body strong and fit. Exercise is good for health. He is doing some exercise.

Expensive

it costs a lot of money to buy it. The bangles were expensive to buy.

Eye

the part of the body with which one sees. Eyes are very important to us, so we have to be careful to look after them.

F is the sixth letter of the English Alphabet.

Face
the front part of your head from your forehead to your chin. Your face shows what you feel.

Fairy
an imaginary creature with magic powers that looks like a tiny person with wings. I love to read fairy tales.

Fall
to drop down. Robby fell down while he was walking.

Family
a group of people related to each other, especially parents and their children. Our family went for a holiday last year.

Fan
a machine or an object that you use to blow or wave air on to you, to keep you cool. Switch on the fan, I am feeling hot.

Farm
an area of land where a farmer grows crops and keeps animals.

Fashion
a style of clothes. Jewellery and clothing fashions vary with the season.

Fast
able to move quickly. This train is going very fast.

Fat
someone who has excessive flesh and plump. Mr. Richard is fat. He eats too much.

Father

a male parent.
My father is a very
honest and noble
man.
He loves me very
much.

Fax

a machine that sends and
receives documents in
an electronic form along
telephone wires and then
prints them.

Feather

one of the light, fluffy
parts that cover a bird's
body. Feathers are soft to
touch.

Fence

something that is built to
separate one area from
another usually made of
wood, stone or wire.
We put up a fence
around our yard.

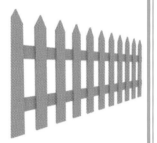

Ferret

an animal that is
used for catching
rats and snakes.

Fight

to engage in
a quarrel, an
argument, or
attempt to harm
someone physically.

Film

roll or sheet of thin
flexible material for
use in photography.

Fingers

long thin parts on
the end of your
hands. There are
four fingers and one
thumb on each hand.

Fire engine

an engine that
has a water tank
and is used to
extinguish fires.

First

being number
one in series.
He is first to
finish the race.

First aid

treatment given
at once to a sick
or injured person
before a doctor
comes.

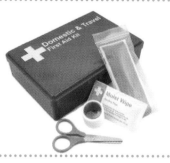

Fish

an animal
that lives and
breathes under
the water.
Fish have fins
and breathe
through gills.

a b c d e **f** g h i j k l m n o p q r s t u v w x y z

Fist
a closed hand when the fingers are rolled in tightly. He banged the table with his fist.

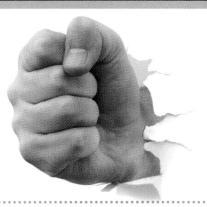

Flag
a piece of cloth decorated with colours and pattern that represent a country, signal or emblem.

Flamingo
a tall long-necked web-footed bird. A flamingo spends its entire life near lakes, marshes, and seas.

Float
to move gently on the surface of water. The small boat floated downstream.

Floor
the lowest flat part of a room. She is cleaning the floor with a broom.

Flower
a coloured part of a plant which produces fruit or seeds.
We planted flowers in the garden.

Flute
a musical device that you play by blowing across a hole near the top. He can play some tunes on the flute.

Fly
a small flying insect. The fly has wings and keeps buzzing around.

Fog
thick mist of water droplets in the air. Heavy fog made it difficult to see the road.

Food
anything you eat to give your body the energy it needs to live and grow. We eat many kinds of food.

Foot
the part forming the lower end of the leg, beginning of the ankle.

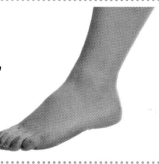

Football
a game played between two teams in which players kick a round ball and try to score a goal. Football is one of the most popular games in the world.

Forest

a large area thickly covered with trees. Many animals live in the forest.

Fork

an instrument with a handle and two or more points, used in eating.

Fountain

a shower of water, pumped up through an ornament into a pool. The crowd gathered around the fountain in the plaza.

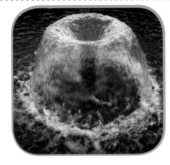

Fox

a small wild animal with red-brown fur, large pointed ears and a bushy tail. A fox looks like a dog.

French Fries

long thin pieces of potato cooked in hot oil. I like to have some French fries with burger.

Fresh

recently made, obtained or arrived. You can use fresh vegetables for this recipe.

Friend

someone you know well and enjoy being with. Linda and Mark are good friends.

Frog

a web-footed animal that moves by jumping and lives on land or in water.

Fruit

The sweet and fleshy product of a tree or other plant that contains seed and can be eaten as food.

Frying pan

a round flat, shallow pan with a long handle, used for frying food.

Full

completely filled. The trolley is full of apples.

Funny

something that makes you laugh. His funny activities amused the kids.

G is the seventh letter of the English Alphabet.

Game

an activity with rules that can be played by one or more people. All kids like to play games.

Gang

a group of people who do things together.

Garbage

unwanted things or waste material, usually from the home. Throw the garbage in the dustbin.

Garden

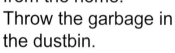

a place where flowers, vegetables, shrubs, etc. are grown. There is a small garden in our backyard.

Garnish

to decorate food to make it look more attractive. Garnish the chicken with coriander and lemon slices.

Gate

a door often made of wood or metal, in an outside wall or fence. Wait for me outside the school gate.

Gift

a thing that you give to someone without payment as a present, especially on a special occasion; a birthday gift.

Giraffe

the tallest mammal, with a long neck and legs and a spotted skin, that feeds on leaves. Giraffes live in Africa.

Girl

a female child or young woman. She is a beautiful and brilliant girl.

Give

to hand over something to the other person. She gave some money to take the parcel.

Glass

a hard, clear substance used in windows, bottles, etc. These bottles and jars are made of glass.

Glasses

something you wear over your eyes to help you see more clearly. I need a new pair of glasses.

Globe

a round ball that has a map on it.
Can you point to where Atlantic Ocean is on the globe?

Glove

a warm or protective hand covering. I have a colourful pair of gloves.

Goat

a farm animal with longer legs, thinner coat and shaggy hair that gives meat and milk.

Goggles

spectacles worn to protect the eyes.

Gold

a very valuable yellow metal used for making jewellery. Gold is a precious metal.

Goldfish

a small fish, often golden, orange in colour, kept in a pool and aquariums.

Goose

a large bird with a long neck and feet that are good for swimming.

Gorilla

a kind of a monkey with no tail. Gorillas have heavy bodies and dark hair.
They eat leaves and other parts of plants.

Grape

a small, round, green or purple fruit which is used for eating or making wine.

a b c d e f g h i j k l m n o p q r s t u v w x y z

g

Grapefruit

a large, yellow citrus fruit with a thick skin and juicy, sour-tasting flesh.

Grasshopper

a jumping insect with long back legs. The grasshopper was hard to see because it was the same colour as the leaf it was sitting on.

Green

the colour of the growing leaves and grass. My favourite colour is green.

Grey

a colour made by mixing black and white. The colour of this dress is grey.

Groom

to clean and brush an animal.

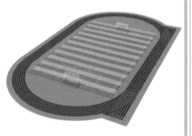

Ground

the solid surface of the Earth, or an area of land used for some purpose.

Group

a number of people or things who are together or connected. It'll be easier if we go there as a group.

Grow

to increase in length, size or amount. The plant grew from a seed.

Guava

a large tropical fruit with pink or white flesh and a lot of seeds. Guava is rich in vitamin C.

Guitar

a musical instrument with strings, played with a pick or with fingers. She plays guitar in a rock band.

Gym

a place where people go to exercise.

H is the eighth letter of the English Alphabet.

Hair
soft thread-like fibres that grow on your head. Girls like long hairs.

Half
one of the two equal parts of something. She cut the apple in half.

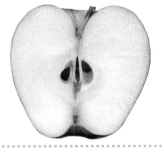

Hall
a large building or a room where people can meet. We rented a hall for the wedding reception.

Hamburger
a type of burger filled with minced meat and other foodstuffs, such as lettuce, tomato, and onion.

Hammer
a tool with a heavy metal head at right angles to the handle, used for breaking stones and driving nails into wood.

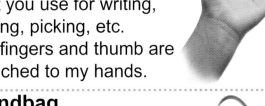

Hand
the part of your body on the end of your arm that you use for writing, eating, picking, etc. My fingers and thumb are attached to my hands.

Handbag
a bag which especially women carry to keep money and other small things.

Handsome
a man who has a very attractive face. He is a handsome man. Everyone likes him.

Happy
feeling pleased and satisfied. The children seem very happy at school.

Hard
solid, firm and not easy to bend, or break. This stone is very hard.

a b c d e f g h i j k l m n o p q r s t u v w x y z h

H

Hat

a piece of clothing that you wear on head. Wear your hat when you are going out in the sun.

Hawk

a bird that looks like an eagle and kills other animals for food. Hawks have sharp claws and a curved beak.

Head

top part of your body where your brain is. James put his hands on his head.

Heart

an organ of the body that pumps blood through the body system. My heart beats faster when I run.

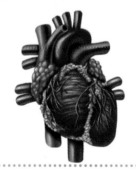

Heater

a machine that heats water or supplies warmth to a room by heating the air in the room.

Heavy

difficult to lift, carry or move. These books are too heavy for me to lift.

Helicopter

a flying machine with large metal blades on the top that spin and lift it into the air.

Helmet

a head-covering worn by cyclists, scooterists, motor cyclists, etc. I always wear a helmet when I ride a bike.

Help

to make something easier for someone or something. It is good to help others.

Hide

to go where you cannot be seen. He is hiding his face.

Hill

a high part of the land, smaller than a mountain. A hill is high ground with sloping sides.

Hip

the part of your body between your thighs and your waist.

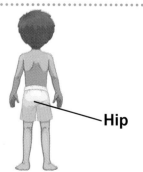

Hip

Hippopotamus

a large, heavy animal with short legs that lives near rivers and lakes in Africa.

Hobby

something that you enjoy doing when you are not working. Jill plays guitar as a hobby.

Hole

an opening in something. There is a big hole in the wall.

Honey

a sweet, sticky, golden-brown food made by bees. She likes honey in her tea.

Hook

a curved piece of metal or plastic used for catching, holding things.

Horse

a large animal which you can ride on or which can be trained to pull loads. Have you ever ridden a horse?

Hospital

a place where sick and injured people get medical treatment.

Hot

having a high temperature. She sipped the coffee. It was very hot.

Hour

a period of time that consists of 60 minutes. The school day is about six hours long.

House

a building where people live. I'd love a house with a garden.

Hug

to hold someone tightly in a loving or caring way. My brother always hugs me before going to school.

Human

any living member belonging to mankind. Humans are very intelligent.

Hungry

feeling that you want to eat. I was so hungry that I ate a lot of fruits.

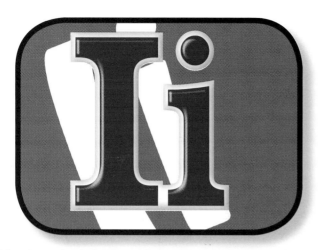

I is the ninth letter of the English Alphabet.

Ice
frozen water. The ice melted quickly in the hot sun.

Ice cream
a sweet food made with cream or milk that has been frozen. I would like to have a chocolate ice cream.

Idea
a thought or a plan. Jose had some good ideas for what he would like for his party.

Idea

Igloo
an Eskimo house made of blocks of hard snow.

Injured
to harm or hurt someone. I injured my hand while cutting vegetables.

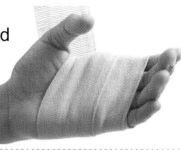

Ink
a coloured liquid used for writing and printing. We are using four different inks for this poster.

Innocent
having little experience of the world, especially of evil or unpleasant things; an innocent child.

Insect
a small living creature whose body has three parts, six legs and usually two pairs of wings to fly.

Inside
inner part of something. The cat is inside the cage.

A B C D E F G H I J K L M N O P Q R S T U V W X Y Z

Instrument
any tool or machine that helps you to do a job.

Internet
the way in which millions of computer around the world are connected and lets people communicate with each other.

Invention
something new that someone makes. The invention of the electric light bulb is attributed to Thomas Alva Edison.

Invite
to ask someone to come to see you or spend some time with you. I invited my friends to my birthday party.

Iron
a flat-bottomed machine that is heated up and used for removing wrinkles and making clothes smooth.

Island
a piece of land that is surrounded by water. There is a small island just off the coast.

Itch
a feeling of irritation on your skin causing you to scratch. I am feeling an itch because of allergy.

Ivy
an evergreen climbing plant, which has pointed leaves. The leaves of ivy are shiny and dark green.

Ivory
the hard white material that the tusks of elephants are made of.

a b c d e f g h i j k l m n o p q r s t u v w x y z

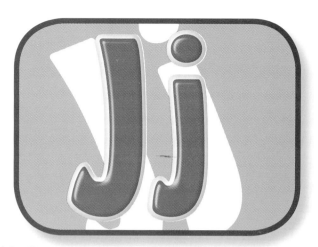

J is the tenth letter of the English Alphabet.

Jackal

a wild dog that is smaller than a wolf. Jackals hunt in packs.

Jacket

something to wear like a coat. I bought a smart leather jacket for myself.

Jaguar

a large, black-spotted cat, found in the forests of tropical America.

Jam

a sweet, sticky food, made from fruit and sugar which you spread on bread. I like mixed-fruit jam.

Jar

a glass container which you use for keeping food in. A jar has a wide top and a lid.

Jasmine

a climbing plant with pink, white or yellow flowers that have sweet smell.

Jaw

one of the two bones between your nose and your chin that hold your teeth. He broke his upper jaw.

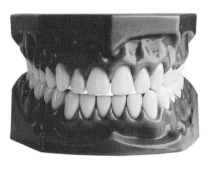

Jeans

trousers made of denim. I bought a new pair of jeans on my birthday.

Jeep

a small strong vehicle, used especially by the armed forces for driving over rough ground.

50

Jelly

a soft, sweet food made of juice of fruit, sugar and water. I like red jelly the best, especially with an ice-cream.

Jellyfish

a sea animal that floats on the surface and can sting. There are different kinds of jellyfish.

Jet

a plane that flies very fast.

Jewel

a precious stone like diamond, ruby, emerald. The diamond is one of world's costliest jewels.

Jigsaw

a picture made of a lot of pieces that you have to fit together. The jigsaw has 100 pieces.

Job

a task that has to be done.
He took a job of a photographer.

Jockey

someone who rides horses in races.

Joey

a baby kangaroo.

Joey

Jog

to run or move along at slow, steady pace. He jogs round the field.

Join

to connect, to put things together.

Joint

a place where two bones are joined together in the body in a way that enables them to bend and move.

Joints

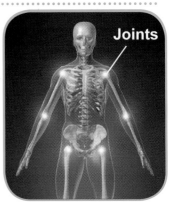

Joke

something that makes you laugh. They all laughed at Ronny's joke.

Journey

a trip from one place to another. I wished him pleasant and safe journey.

Joy

feeling of great happiness. We shouted with joy when our team got selected.

Joystick

a lever used for playing computer games. The boy held the joystick tightly in his hand.

Judo

a Japanese fighting sport. In judo, people try to throw each other to the floor.

Jug

a container with a lip for pouring liquid. Put a jug of milk on the table.

Juice

the liquid that comes from fruit, often used as a drink. We had an orange juice in the morning.

Jump

to go into the air. The horse jumped and crossed the river.

Jungle

a place that has a lot of trees and plants growing in it. Monkeys live in jungles.

Junk food

food that is not healthy. Potato chips, cola, or other snacks that are high in fat are known as junk food.

Jute

a strong fibre that comes from a tropical plant and is used for making rope and bags.

K is the eleventh letter of the English Alphabet.

Kangaroo

a large animal that moves by jumping. Kangaroo has strong back legs, and carries a baby in a pocket on their stomach.

Karate

a Japanese form of self-defense in which sharp, quick blows are struck with the hands and feet.

Kayak

a light canoe in which the part where you sit is covered over. A kayak moves through the water by paddling.

Kebab

a food consisting of small pieces of meat and vegetables cooked on a stick. I like to have chicken kebab in snacks.

Kennel

a small shelter for dogs or cats. I have a special kennel for my dog.

Ketchup

a thick smooth-textured sauce usually made from tomatoes and eaten with snacks.

Kettle

a vessel usually made from metal used for boiling or cooking. Put the kettle on and make some tea.

Key

a special piece of metal used to open a lock. Turn the key to the left.

Keyboard

a set of keys on a computer, piano, etc. This is a special keyboard with pictures and letters.

Kick

to hit something with foot. When you kick you move your legs. Jackson gave the ball a powerful kick.

Kid

(a) a child. A group of kids is reading books.
(b) a young goat.

Kidney

the organ in the body that removes waste products from the blood and produces urine.

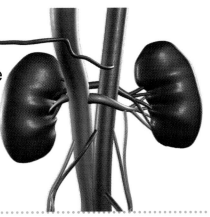

Kind

a gentle, friendly and generous person who cares about others. Rocky is very kind and helpful to animals.

King

a royal man who rules a territory. The king lives in a palace and takes care of his subjects.

Kingdom

a territory that has a king or queen as a leader. The king loved all the people of his kingdom.

Kingfisher

a blue and orange bird that lives near water and eats fish.

Kiss

to touch someone with your lips. Peter kissed his mother because he loves her.

Kit

a box or bag for carrying a set of tool or other items.

Kitchen

a room in a house for preparing food. Keep all the utensils in the kitchen.

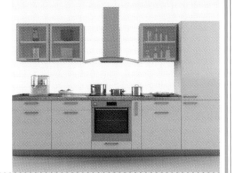

Kite

a toy that flies in the air while you hold it by a long string. The children like to fly kites on windy days.

Kitten

a baby cat. Our cat had four kittens.

Knee

the part in the middle of your leg that bends. Lucy is sitting on her knees.

Knife

a tool with a blade that is used for cutting things in pieces. You need a sharp knife to cut this.

Knock

to hit something, a door or window with your hand. William knocked at the door, but nobody answered.

Knot

a part where two pieces of string or rope are tied together.

Koala

an Australian animal with grey fur, large ears and no tail. Lots of people think that koalas are bears, but they are not.

Kohlrabi

a vegetable of cabbage family, whose thick round white stem is eaten.

Komodo dragon

a very large lizard from Indonesia.

Kumquat

a fruit like a very small orange with sweet skin that is eaten, and sour pulp.

a b c d e f g h i j k l m n o p q r s t u v w x y z

K

L is the twelfth letter of the English Alphabet.

Lace
a fine cloth made with patterns of many small holes.

Ladder
a structure for climbing up or down that consist of two long bars joined together by small pieces called rungs.

Lady
a woman.
Jane is an attractive young lady.

Ladybug
a small round, flying beetle. The back of a ladybug is brightly coloured with black spots.

Lake
a big area of water that is surrounded by land.
There are plentiful fish in the lake.

Lamb
a baby sheep.
Lambs are born in the spring.

Lamp
a kind of a light, that stands on a desk or table. Use a lamp when you study.

Land
the solid dry area of the Earth's surface that is not sea.

Lane
a narrow road or street in the country.

Lantern

a case of glass, or other material that holds a light or flame. You can carry a lantern.

Large

big in size, amount, or number. There is a large tree near the road side.

Last

after all the others. Letter Z comes last in the English alphabet.

Latch

a simple fastening for a door, window, or gate.

Laugh

to make sounds with your voice, when you are very happy or when you think that something is funny. John laughed when he was playing.

Laundry

clothes, sheets, etc. that need to be washed or have just been washed. She did the laundry before leaving for work.

Lawn

a place in a garden or a park with grass that has been cut very short. The kids had their lunch in the lawn.

Lazy

someone who doesn't like to work. He is the laziest boy in the class.

Leaf

a flat green part of a plant. The trees drop their leaves in the fall, and new leaves grow again in the spring.

Learn

to gain knowledge or a skill. I learned cycling from my father.

Leek

a vegetable with a long white stem and long flat green leaves, which tastes like an onion.

Leg

one of the parts of a person or animal's body which is used for support and for walking. A young boy is lying on the floor with his legs facing upwards.

a b c d e f g h i j k l m n o p q r s t u v w x y z

Lemon

a yellow citrus fruit with a thick skin and juicy, sour pulp.

Lemonade

a drink made with lemon juice, sugar and water.
A glass of lemonade.

Leopard

a large strong cat that has yellow fur with black spots. Leopards are found in Africa and Asia.

Letter

a message that you write to someone, or receive from someone.
Hannah writes a letter to me every week.

Lettuce

a green leafy vegetable eaten in salads. I like lettuce in my food.

Lid

a cover for something, such as a pot, can or bottle that can be opened. He opened the lid of the can with an opener.

Lid

Light

the energy from the sun, a flame, a lamp, etc. that allows you see things. Turn on the light, it's too dark.

Lighthouse

a tower or other structure containing a beacon light to warn or guide ships at sea. A lighthouse was put up near the coast.

Lightning

a flash of bright light in the sky during a thunderstorm.

Like

to be happy with or to be fond of something. She likes to eat apple.

Limb

an arm or a leg of a human being. My limbs are fit and strong.

Line

a long thin mark usually on a piece of paper. Draw a straight line with a pen.

Lion

a large wild animal with golden fur. Lion is the king of all animals.

Lips
the upper and lower soft edges of your mouth.
Her thin red lips stretched into a smile.

Lipstick
something used for adding colour to your lips, in the shape of a small stick.

Liquid
a substance that flows freely and is not a solid or a gas, for example water or oil.
There is a liquid soap in the bottle.

List
to set down words, numbers, etc. in a line.
I am making a list of people, whom I have to invite.

Little
small in size. A little boy is playing with a little dog.

Liver
a large organ of the body that is near the stomach.
Liver cleans the blood.

Livestock
cattle, horses, sheep, or other animals kept and raised on a farm.

Lizard
a small reptile with long, thin body and tail.

Llama
a South American animal with thick hair like wool, and a long neck.

Lobster
a sea animal with eight legs and two claws.

Lock
a part of a door, box, etc. that you can open and shut with a key.
Lock the door properly before leaving.

a b c d e f g h i j k l m n o p q r s t u v w x y z

Log

a thick piece of wood that is cut from or has fallen from a tree.

Lollipop

a hard candy on the end of a stick. Kids love to eat lollipops.

Long

measuring a great length.
He stretched out his long legs.

Look

turn one's eyes in some direction.
Jessie looked carefully for some change in her purse.

Looking glass

a mirror made of glass.
She looked at herself through a looking glass.

Lost

not knowing where you are or you cannot find your way.
My dog got lost in the market.

Love

to have a strong feeling of liking someone.
I love my sister very much.

Lovebird

a small brightly coloured parrot that is often kept as a pet in a cage.

Lunch

the meal that people eat in the middle of the day.
Let's meet for lunch.

Lung

two organs inside your chest that you use to breathe.

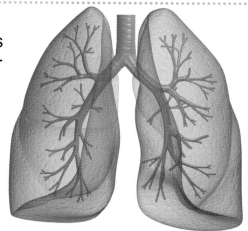

Lychee

a small Chinese fruit with thick rough reddish skin, white flesh and a large seed inside.

M is the thirteenth letter of the English Alphabet.

Macaw

a large, bright coloured parrot of Central and South America. Macaws have a long tail and a harsh cry.

Machine

something that is made up of moving parts and is often run by electricity.

Magazine

a book with a paper cover that contains news stories, articles, photographs, etc. and is sold weekly or monthly.

Magician

a person who does magic tricks. The magician entertained everyone with his tricks.

Magnet

a piece of iron or certain other materials that attract objects made of iron towards it, either naturally or because of an electric current that is passed through it.

Magnify

to make a thing appear larger than it is. I use a magnifying lens to make things appear larger.

Magpie

a long-tailed bird with a boldly marked plumage and a noisy cry.

Maid

a girl or woman who is paid to do housework. I have a maid to do the housework.

Mall

a large area where there are a lot of shops, stores, restaurants, etc. inside it. The food court at the shopping mall is always full.

Mammal

an animal that feed its young on its own milk. Human, cows, dogs and cats are all mammals.

Man

an adult male human being.
He is a very kind man.

Mango

a sweet yellow fruit from a tree that grow in hot countries.
I love the taste of mangoes.

Map

a detailed plan of an area, showing features like towns, roads, mountains, etc.
We studied the map of world.

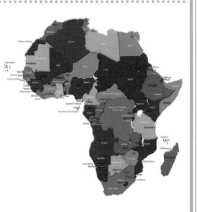

Marble

(a) a small glass ball that is used to play a game. (b) a hard stone that is usually white, used for sculpture and as building material.

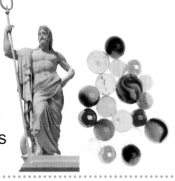

Mark

to write or draw a symbol, line, etc. on something in order to give information about it.

Market

an open place, or a building with stalls where goods are sold. We buy our fruit and vegetables at the market.

Mask

a covering worn over a face to hide or protect it.
The dancers wore colourful masks.

Mat

a piece of rough material that covers a floor or other surface.
Do not wipe your feet on the mat.

Maze

a children's game in which you try to draw a line through a complicated group of lines without crossing any of them.

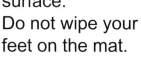

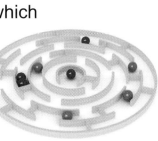

Meal

a time when you eat food, for example breakfast, lunch, or dinner or the food that you eat at one of these times.

Medal

a small, flat piece of metal that has a design or some words on it. Medals are given to someone who has won a competition or who has done something brave.

Medicine

something that you take when you are not well so that you will get better.
He forgot to take his medicine.

Melt

to change from a solid to a liquid by heat.
The candle wax began to melt after some time.

Menu

a list of all the kinds of food that are available for a meal, especially in a restaurant. The menu has a good choice of desserts.

Mermaid

an imaginary sea creature.
The head and upper body of a mermaid is of a woman and the lower body has a tail of a fish.

Merry-Go-Round

a machine that turns around and around, and has model animals or cars for children to sit on.

Metal

a hard, shiny material like silver, iron or copper. The frame is made of metal.

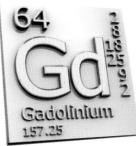

Microscope

something that makes small things look much bigger. Students viewed the crystals through a microscope.

Microwave

an oven that is used to heat or prepare food quickly.
Put the pasta in microwave for three minutes.

Middle

the centre or the part of something that is between the beginning and end.
Johnny is sitting in the middle.

Midnight
the time in the middle of the night when it is 12 o' clock. It was 12 midnight when we arrived home.

Milk
a white liquid that female human and other mammals produce to feed their babies. I always drink a glass of milk in the morning.

Mill
a building fitted with machines that produce a particular type of material; a cloth mill, a paper mill.

Mint
a small plant with a green leaves used for cooking.

Minute
a small measure of time, 60 seconds long. Bake the cake for 25–30 minutes.

Mirror
a looking-glass. I looked at myself in the mirror.

Mix
to put the things together. Mix all the ingredients properly.

Money
the coins or piece of paper which you use to pay for the things you buy. You will find some money in my bag.

Monkey
a furry animal with a long tail and strong arms. Monkeys live in hot countries.

Monster
an imaginary creature that is big and frightening. Monsters are large and ugly.

Month
one of twelve periods into which a year is divided.

January	Sun	Mon	Tue	Wed	Thu	Fri	Sat
		1	2	3	4	5	6	7
	8	9	10	11	12	13	14
	15	16	17	18	19	20	21
	22	23	24	25	26	27	28
	29	30	31				

Moon

a round object that you can see as a light in the sky at night. The moon moves around the Earth every 28 days.

Morning

the time from sunrise to noon. We spent the morning walking in the park.

Mother

a female parent. Mother loves her children. I love my mother very much.

Mountain

a very high part of the earth. There was still snow on the mountain tops.

Mouse

a small furry animal that has sharp teeth and a long tail. A mouse has pointed nose.

Mouth

the part of your face below your nose that you use to eat and speak. The human mouth contains the tongue, teeth, and lips.

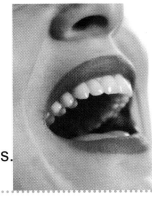

Mug

a large cup with a handle. I have a collection of coffee mugs.

Muscle

one of the pieces of flesh that connects to the bones in your body that helps to make your body move. My brother goes to the gym to build up his muscles.

Mushroom

a small vegetable that has a stem with a round top. We had mushroom soup before dinner.

Musician

someone who performs or writes music. These young musicians are very talented.

a b c d e f g h i j k l m n o p q r s t u v w x y z

65

N is the fourteenth letter of the English Alphabet.

Nail
one of the hard parts that grow at the end of your fingers and toes.
Don't bite your nails it's a bad manners.

Naked
without any clothes on.

Name
what someone or something is called.
My name is Maria.

Nap
to sleep for a short time.
I took a nap after having my lunch.

Napkin
a piece of cloth or paper used at meals for protecting your clothes and cleaning your lips and fingers.

Nappy
a piece of towelling or other absorbent material wrapped around a baby's bottom.

Naughty
a person, usually a child who does not obey and behaves badly.

Navel
the small hollow or raised place in the middle of your stomach.

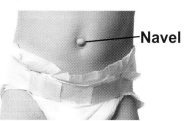

Navel

Neat
something that is tidy and ordered. His room is always neat and tidy.

Neck
the part of the body connecting the head to the shoulders.

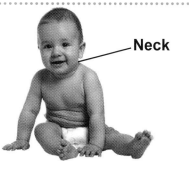

Neck

Necklace

a piece of jewellery worn around your neck. Wow! What a pretty necklace.

Needle

a pointed thin sharp metal with a slit for thread, used in sewing.

Nest

a place where a bird lays eggs and shelters it's young. See the bird's nest high up in the tree.

Net

something used for catching fish, insects, or animals which is made of threads or wires woven across each other with regular spaces between them.

Newspaper

a printed publication containing news, articles, advertisement, etc. and published everyday or every week.

Nice

pleasant, enjoyable or attractive. Dave, you look nice in suit.

Night

the time from sunset to sunrise. It is a dark night

Nightingale

a small bird known for the beautiful way that it sings at night.

Noise

a loud sound, often unpleasant. Don't make a loud noise.

Noodles

very thin pasta in long pieces that you can put in soups, Chinese dishes, etc.

a b c d e f g h i j k l m n o p q r s t u v w x y z

Noon

12 o' clock in the daytime; midday.
The meeting will take place from noon to 3 p.m.

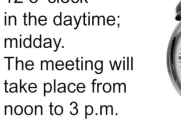

North

the direction that is on your left when you are looking at the sun when it rises, and usually at the top of the map.

Nose

the part of your face that you use for smelling and breathing.
Breathe in deeply through your nose.

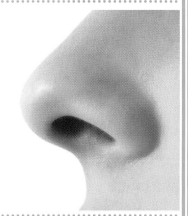

Notebook

a small book of paper, used for writing notes.
Kelly wrote down what the teacher said in her notebook.

Notice

to see or become aware of something.

Novel

a book that tells a story.
I love reading novels.

Number

a word or sign used for counting and doing sums.

Nurse

a woman who takes care of sick people in a hospital.
Sara is a nurse in the City hospital.

Nursery School

a school for children who are between three and five years old.

Nut

a dry fruit with a hard shell.
Peanuts, cashew nuts, and almonds are different types of nuts.

O is the fifteenth letter of the English Alphabet.

Oak tree
a large tree with hard wood.

Oatmeal
a soft breakfast food made by boiling crushed oats.

Obedient
dutifully complying with orders or requests;
doing what you are told to do.

Obese
very fat, in a way that is dangerous for your health.

Object
something that you can see and touch, but is not alive.

Ocean
one of the large areas of water on the Earth's surface. The map shows the five main oceans of the world.

Ocelot
a large American wild cat that has a pattern of spots on its back.

Octopus
a sea creature with a soft round body and eight long thin parts like arms that are sometimes used for food.

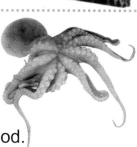

Odd
something that is unusual or strange.

Office
a place where people work at desks, writing and making telephone calls, or working on computers.

a b c d e f g h i j k l m n o p q r s t u v w x y z

Oil

a smooth thick liquid that is made from plants or animals and is used in cooking: Olive oil, vegetable oil.

Ointment

a soft cream that you rub into your skin, especially as a medical treatment.

Old

having been used for a long time. This is an old football.

Olive

a small green or black fruit with a strong taste, used in cooking and for its oil.

Omelette

a food you make by mixing eggs together and cooking them in a pan, sometimes other food added. Let us have a cheese omelette with a French toast for breakfast.

Onion

a vegetable with a strong smell and flavour. Chop the onions finely.

Open

not shut or locked. The briefcase is open and empty.

Opossum

one of various small animals from America and Australia that have fur and climb trees.

Orange

a round fruit with a thick, orange skin and sweet, juicy flesh. I want to have orange juice.

Orangutan

a large ape with long arms and long orange-brown hair.

Orchard
a place where fruit trees are grown.

Orchestra
a large group of people who play musical instruments together.

Origami
the Japanese art of folding paper into decorative shapes and figures.

Oriole
a bird having bright yellow and black plumage that feed on fruit and insects.

Ornament
a small, attractive object that you use to decorate.

Ostrich
a large African swift-running flightless bird. Ostriches cannot fly.

Oval
egg shaped. The wall-clock is oval in shape.

Oven
an electronic machine that is used for baking or roasting food. Bake the cake in the oven.

Overcoat
a long thick warm coat. An overcoat is worn in cold weather.

Owl
a bird with large eyes, that hunts at night. Owls have soft feathers and a hooked beak.

Ox
a large adult male cattle used for ploughing, pulling carts, etc.

Oyster
a shellfish with a hard shell and a soft body that can be eaten.

abcdefghijklmnopqrstuvwxyz

P is the sixteenth letter of the English Alphabet.

Pacifier

a nipple of rubber or other material that is given to babies to suck on.

Pack

a container usually made of paper that holds a number of the same thing or an amount of something, ready to be sold.

Paddle

a short oar that has a wide blade at one or both ends.

Pail

a round, deep container, usually with a handle, for holding and carrying liquids, sand, and other things.

Pain

the feeling you have when part of your body hurts.
She has a pain in her neck.

Paint

a coloured liquid material that is used to paint walls and furniture.

Pair

(a) two people or animals a male and a female animal that come together.
(b) a set of two similar things which are used or worn together.

Palace

the home of a person of very high rank, especially a king or queen.
A palace is a large, grand building.

Palette

a thin board with a hole in it for the thumb to go through, used by an artist for mixing colours on when painting.

Palm

the inner surface of the hand between the wrist and fingers.

Panda

a black and white animal that looks like a bear.
Panda lives in the mountains of China.

Panther

a large wild animal that is black and a member of the cat family.

Papa

a way of talking to or about your father.
Papa is a word used mainly by children.

Papaya

a fruit with yellow and green skin, sweet orange or red flesh and round black seeds.

Paper

a thin sheet used for writing, drawing or printing on.
Write it down on a piece of paper.

Parachute

an umbrella shaped apparatus allowing a person or heavy object, attached to it, to fall slowly from a height.

Parakeet

a small, slender parrot with a long tail.
Parakeets are often kept as pets.

Parcel

goods etc. wrapped up in a single package.

Parent

the father or mother of a person or animal.
Joe and Jennie live with their parents.

Park

a large public garden in a city, for recreation.

Parrot

a colourful bird with a short hooked bill, often able to mimic the human voice.
Parrots are kept as pets.

Partridge

a fat brown bird with a short tail which is shot for sport and food.

a b c d e f g h i j k l m n o p q r s t u v w x y z

p

Party

a social gathering, usually of invited guests.

Pasta

an Italian food made from flour, water and sometimes eggs, formed into different shapes and usually served with a sauce. It is hard when dry and soft when cooked.

Paste

a soft thick mixture that can easily be shaped or spread. Paste is moist and smooth.

Pastry

a small cake, a single pie, or other baked food. I love eating pastry.

Paw

the foot of an animal having claws or nails. This kitten has a sore paw.

Pea

a small round green seed which grows inside a pod, eaten as food.

Peach

a round juicy fruit with a large stone inside. The peach is orange-yellow, sweet and juicy fruit.

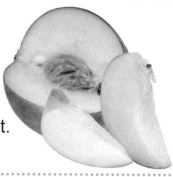

Peacock

a large bird, the male of which has long blue and green tail feathers that it can lift up and spread out.

Peanut

a small nut with a pod that ripens underground.

Pearl

a precious stone or jewel found inside the shells of some oysters.

Peel

to cut away or pull off the skin or rind of fruit, vegetables, etc.

Pelican
a water bird with a large bill and a pouch in the throat for storing fish.

Pen
an instrument for writing in ink. This is a fountain pen.

Pencil
an instrument that you use for writing or drawing, consisting of a wooden stick with a thin piece of a black or coloured substance in the middle.

Pendant
a locket, or other ornament that hangs down.

Penguin
a flightless black and white sea bird that is found in cold places.
Penguins use their wings to help them swim.

Pepper
a hot-tasting seasoning made by grinding the dried berries of a tropical plant.

Perfume
a liquid with a pleasing smell that is put on the body.

Pet
a domestic or tamed animal kept for pleasure or companionship. The dog is a pet animal.

Petal
a brightly coloured part that looks like leaf and make up the flower of a plant. Rose petals are very smooth to touch.

Pheasant
a wild bird with a long, sweeping tail and brightly coloured feathers. Pheasant is hunted as game.

Photograph
a picture that is taken by using a camera.
Betty took a photograph of Tom.

Piano
a large musical instrument with black and white keys that one presses down to make sounds.
A piano has 88 keys.

Pickle
a vegetable or fruit that has been preserved in vinegar or salt water and has a strong flavour, served cold with meat, salads, etc.

a b c d e f g h i j k l m n o p q r s t u v w x y z

Picnic

a pleasure trip away from home during which a meal is eaten outdoors.
We all enjoyed the picnic by the river.

Piece

one of the parts that something divides or breaks into.
The pizza was cut into four pieces.

Pigeon

a fast flying bird used as a pet.
Most pigeons are grey, but some are white.

Pile

a number of things that have been placed on top of each other.

Pillow

a soft pad used to rest the head on it in sleeping.

Pilot

a person who operates the flying controls of an aircraft.

Pineapple

a juicy fruit that consists of yellow flesh surrounded by a tough segmented skin and topped with a tuft of stiff leaves.
Pineapple juice is sweet.

Pink

a pale red colour. This rose is pink.

Pirate

a person on a ship who attacks other ships at sea in order to steal things they are carrying.

Pizza

an Italian dish consisting of a flat round bread base with cheese, tomatoes, vegetables, meat, etc. on top.

Planet

a very large round object in space that moves around the sun or another star.

Plate

a circular vessel from which food is eaten or served.
This is a dinner plate.

Pray

to address a diety, a prophet, a saint, or an object of worship especially to ask for help or give thanks.

Q is the seventeenth letter of the English Alphabet.

Quail

a small fat bird with a short tail that is hunted for food or sport.

Quarrel
an angry argument. They had a quarrel about money.

Quarter

one of the four equal parts.
Cut the apple into quarters.

Quartz

a hard mineral, often in crystal form, that is used to make very accurate clocks and watches.

Queasy

feeling sick; wanting to vomit.
Mona began to feel queasy.

Queen

a woman from a royal family, who is the ruler of her country. Cleopatra was the queen of Egypt.

Question

the thing you say or write when you ask someone something. Marry wrote answers of all the questions in her notebook.

Queue

a line of people or vehicle waiting for something.
They stood in a queue for half an hour.

Quick

able to move fast or do something fast.
Go and get the parcel delivered quickly.

Quiet

no noise or sound.
Shh! Keep quiet.

Quiz

a competition or game in which people try to answer questions to test their knowledge.

R is the eighteenth letter of the English Alphabet.

Rabbit

a small animal with long ears and soft fur that some people keep as a pet.

Raccoon

a small North American animal with black fur around its eyes and black and grey rings on its tail.

Race

a competition that decides who is fastest at doing something.

Racket

a piece of sports equipment used for hitting the ball, etc. in the games of tennis, squash or badminton. It has an oval frame, with strings stretched across and down it.

Radio

a machine which you turn on to hear news, entertainment or music.

Radish

a small vegetable whose red or white root is eaten raw and has a strong spicy taste.

Raft

a floating platform made by tying long pieces of wood together, used as a boat.

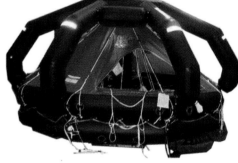

Rag

a piece of old, often torn, cloth used especially for cleaning things.

Rain

the water that falls from the sky in drops. Plants grow well when there is a lot of rain.

Raindrop
a drop of rain.
There are rain
drops on the
window panes.

Raincoat
a coat that you wear
to protect yourself
from rain.
A raincoat is a
waterproof coat.

Raisin
a dried grape,used
in cakes, etc.

Rake
a gardening tool with a
long handle and long
prongs.
A rake is used for
making soil level,
gathering up dead
leaves, etc.

Rat
an animal like a
mouse, with a
long tail and sharp
teeth.

Rattle
an instrument
that is
shaken to
amuse a
baby.

Raven
a large shiny
black bird of the
crow family.
Raven has a rough
unpleasant cry.

Reach
to stretch out the
hand for something.
The child is trying to
reach the cherries.

Read
to look at and
understand words
in a letter, book,
newspaper, etc.
Jenny loves reading
mystery stories.

Receive
to get or
to accept
something.

r

Recipe

a set of instructions for cooking or preparing a particular food.

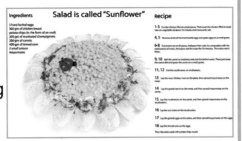

Rectangle

a plane figure with four straight sides and four right angles.

Recycle

to change the waste material like glass bottles, newspapers, so that they can be used again.

Red

the colour of blood or a similar colour.

Refrigerator

a large container that is kept cool inside with electricity and is used for keeping food and cold drinks.

Relax

to rest and allow yourself to be comfortable.

Reptile

a cold-blooded egg-laying animal that creeps and crawls.

Reindeer

a large deer with long horns shaped like branches that lives in cold northern regions.

Restaurant

a room or a building where you buy a meal and eat it. He went to a restaurant for lunch.

Rhinoceros

a large heavy animal with very thick skin and either one or two horns on its nose that lives in Africa and Asia.

80

Ribbon

a long, thin piece of material that you use for tying things up or make something look pretty.

Rice

a grain that is boiled and eaten as food.

Ride

to sit on a horse, bicycle, or motorcycle and travel along it. She arrived riding on a horse.

Ring

a circle of metal that you wear on your finger.

Rise

to get up from a lying, sitting or kneeling position.

River

the long area of water going through the land.

Road

a track for vehicles like cars buses and trucks to travel along.

Roar

to make a very loud, deep sound. We heard a lion roar.

Robin

a bird with a red chest. A robin is a small bird. The back of the robin is brown.

Robot

a machine which does a job that is usually done by a person. This is a toy robot.

a b c d e f g h i j k l m n o p q r s t u v w x y z

Rock

the very hard substance of which the Earth is made.

Rocket

a long vehicle for travelling in space.

Roof

the covering on the top of a building. A roof is usually supported by its walls.

Rooster

an adult male chicken.

Rope

a strong, very thick string that can be used for tying or pulling things.

Rose

a garden flower that often has a sweet smell and grows on bushes with thorns.

Round

shaped like a circle or ball.

Rubber

a tough elastic substance made from the latex of plants. Rubber is used in making erasers, car tyres and many other things.

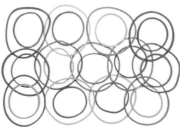

Rug

a floor-mat of thick material, usually smaller than a carpet.

Ruler

an object used for measuring or for drawing straight lines, consisting of long, thin piece of wood marked with units of measurements.

Run

to move quickly or to go faster than a walk, using your legs. Run as fast as you can, or else you will miss your bus.

S is the nineteenth letter of the English Alphabet.

Sack
a large bag with no handles, made of strong rough material or strong paper or plastic, used for storing and carrying, for example flour, coal, etc.

Sad
to be unhappy. David is sad because he lost his ball.

Saddle
a leather seat fastened on a horse for riding. This is an old saddle.

Sail
a piece of material used for catching the wind and propelling a boat or ship.

Salad
a kind of cold food usually made with raw vegetables and fresh fruit.

Salt
a white substance that is added to food to give it a better flavour or to preserve it. Add some more salt in the soup.

Sand
very small pieces of rock that you find on beaches and deserts.

Sandals
open shoes worn in warm weather.

Sandwich
two pieces of bread with a filling in between.

Sauce
a thick liquid that is eaten with food to add flavour to it.

a b c d e f g h i j k l m n o p q r s t u v w x y z

S

Scarecrow

a figure in the shape of a person that a farmer puts in a field to frighten birds away.

Scared

frightened. John got scared when he saw a scorpion.

Scarf

a piece of clothing that you wrap around the neck or head.

School

a place where children go to study and are taught.

Scientist

a person whose job is to do work using science. Scientists do experiments.

Scissors

a tool for cutting paper, cloth, etc. made of two sharp blades fastened together in the middle, with holes for your finger and thumb.

Scorpion

a small poisonous stinging animal. Scorpions live in hot countries.

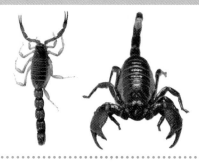

Scream

to cry out loudly usually when you are angry, afraid, or hurt.

Sea

a large area of salty water that covers most of the earth's surface.

Seal

a fish-eating sea mammal with flippers and webbed feet. Seals are good swimmers.

Seasons

one of the main periods into which a year is divided, which each have a particular type of weather. There are four seasons in the year: winter, spring, summer, and fall (also called autumn).

Secret

some information that people keep to themselves and hide from others.

84

See

observe; look at. If I shut my eyes, I cannot see.

Seed

the small hard part produced by a plant from which a new plant can grow. Sow seed in May or June.

Seesaw

a piece of equipment for children to play on consisting of a long flat piece of wood that is supported in the middle. A child sits at each end and makes the seesaw move up and down.

Shadow

a dark figure made by a body when it gets in the way of a ray of light.

Shampoo

a liquid soap for washing hair. A bottle of shampoo.

Share

to let someone else have a part of something you have. Jack shared his glass of milkshake with Michael.

Shark

a large fish with sharp teeth.

Sharp

something that has fine pointed edge and makes it easy to cut things with it. This knife is sharp.

Shawl

a large piece of cloth worn especially by women over the shoulders or head.

Sheep

an animal with a thick coat, kept on farms for its meat or its wool.

a b c d e f g h i j k l m n o p q r s t u v w x y z

S

Shell

the hard outer covering of a small creature that lives in the sea. Shells are often found at the beach.

Ship

a large boat that carries many people and goods over the sea.

Shirt

a piece of clothing that you wear to cover the top half of your body.

Shoe

covering for foot made of leather, canvas, etc.

Shop

a place where you can buy goods or services.

Shopping

the things you buy by going to a shop or shops.

Short

not long or tall; smaller than usual. Turtle is a short-necked creature that lives in water and on land.

Shoulder

the part of your body below your neck.

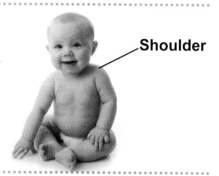

Shoulder

Shower

to wash yourself using a shower. It's too hot, I need a shower.

Shrub

a woody plant that is smaller than a tree and has a number of stems instead of one trunk.

Sick

not well, people who are physically or mentally ill.

Silence

not speaking or making any noise. 'Silence in the class!' said the teacher.

Silver

a white shiny metal used in jewellery and coins.

Sing

to make musical sounds with the voice. She sings beautifully.

Size

how big or small something is. Let me measure the size.

Skate

sports equipment with a thin blade on the bottom or small wheels attached to the bottom that is worn on feet for moving on ice or ground.

Skateboard

a short narrow board with small wheels at each end, which you stand on and ride as a sport.

Skeleton

the bony framework that supports the body of a person or an animal. The human skeleton consists of about 206 bones.

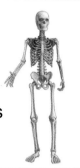

Sketch

a simple quickly made picture that does not have many details.

Ski

one of a pair of long, narrow pieces of wood, metal, or plastic attached to boots used for moving smoothly over snow.

Skin

the thin layer of tissues that covers the body of a person or animal.

Skirt

a female's piece of clothing that hangs from the waist.

Sky

the space above the Earth where clouds and the Sun and stars appear.

Skyscraper

a very tall building.

Sled

a vehicle for carrying loads or persons over snow.

Sleep

to rest with your eyes closed and the mind and body is not active.

Slice

a thin broad piece cut from something. A slice of bread.

Slim

attractively thin. She is tall and slim.

Small

not large in size or amount. This slide is too small but contains a lot of information.

Smell

the ability to sense different things by using nose. The smell of perfume is very pleasant.

Smile

an expression of the face that shows you are happy. John smiled broadly when he saw his mother.

Snail

a small creature that moves very slowly and has a hard shell on its back.

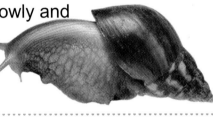

Snake

a reptile with a long thin body and no legs. There are many types of snakes; some of them have a poisonous bite.

Snow

small soft white pieces of frozen water that fall from the sky in cold weather.

Snowman

a simple figure of a person made of snow, made especially by children.

Soap

a substance that you use with water for washing your body.

Sock

a piece of clothing made of soft material that is worn over the foot, especially inside a shoe.

Sofa

a long comfortable seat with a back and arms, for two or more people to sit on.

Soft

not hard; smooth and pleasant to touch. The furry toy was soft to the touch.

Soft drink

a drink that does not contain alcohol and usually is carbonated.

Sorry

feeling sad and ashamed about something that has been done.

Soup

a liquid food that is made by cooking meat, fish, or vegetables, etc. in water. A bowl of soup.

Sour

having a sharp, acid taste like that of a lemon or of fruit that is not ready to eat.

Space

the amount of an area room, container that is available for use.

Space craft

a vehicle used for travelling in space.

Sparrow

common, small grey and brown songbird with short beak.

Spectacles
a pair of eye glasses that help you to see. Spectacles help Sam to see well.

Spell
to write or say the letters of a word in correct order.

Spider
a small creature with eight thin legs. Many spiders spin webs.

Spin
to turn round and round quickly. Give the wheel a spin.

Spinach
the vegetable with large, dark green leaves that are eaten raw or cooked.

Sponge
a piece of a soft natural or artificial substance full of small holes, which can suck up liquid and is used for washing.

Spoon
an object that you use for eating, cooking, or serving food.

Sport
an activity or a game that you play for exercise or pleasure. My favourite sports are swimming and badminton.

Sprain
to injure a joint in your body, especially your wrist or ankle, by suddenly twisting it.

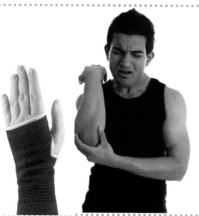

Spray
a substance that is forced out of a container such as an aerosol, in very small drops.

Spring

a twisted piece of metal that will return to its previous shape after it has been pressed down.

Square

a shape having four straight equal sides and four right angles.

Squash

a type of vegetable that grows on the ground. Winter squash have hard skin and orange flesh.
Summer squash have soft yellow or green skin and white flesh.

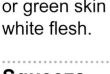

Squeeze

to press hard especially with your fingers or hand.

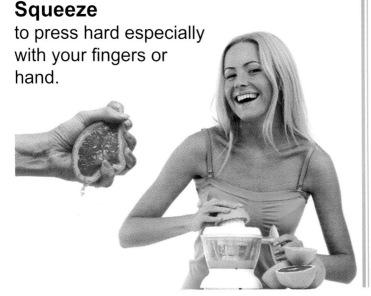

Squirrel

a small animal with a long furry tail that lives in trees and eats nuts.

Stairs

a set of steps built between two floors inside a building that go up or down.

Stamp

(a) a piece of paper that you buy to put on an envelope or a package before you post it.

(b) a thing you put ink on and then press onto something to make a mark.

Stand

have an upright position, especially on the feet.
The school girl is standing and waiting for her friends.

a b c d e f g h i j k l m n o p q r s t u v w x y z

S

Stapler

a tool used to staple papers together.

Star

a large ball of burning gas in space that shines by its own light and can be seen at night in the sky.

Starfish

a small sea animal that has five arms forming the shape of a star. Starfish move very slowly.

Stationery

materials that you use for writing, such as paper, pens, pencils, etc.

Statue

an image of a person or animal that is made in solid material such as stone or metal and is usually large.

Steel

a strong hard metal that is made of a mixture of iron and carbon.

Stick

a long thin piece of wood, plastic, etc. that you use for a particular purpose.

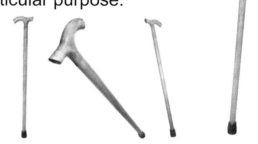

Stir

to move or shake something slightly using a spoon in order to mix it thoroughly.

Stomach

the organ inside the body where food goes when you swallow it; the front part of the body below the chest.

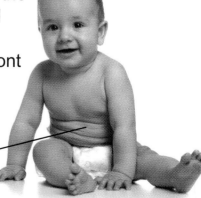

Stomach

Stone
hard material that is found in the ground, often used for building. Most of the houses are built of stone.

Stop
to make someone not walk, move or travel.

Stork
a tall white bird with long legs and a long beak. Storks are often found wading in shallow water.

Store
a place where you go to buy things.

Storm
a strong wind along with heavy rain, snow, or hail, often with thunder and lightning.

Story
a description of how something happened, that is intended to entertain people, and may be true or imaginary.

Straw
a hollow tube that is used to drink liquids.

Strawberry
a soft red juicy fruit with small seeds on its surface.

Student
a person who is studying at a school or college.

Submarine
a type of ship, especially a military one that can travel underwater.

a b c d e f g h i j k l m n o p q r s t u v w x y z

Success

the result that you have achieved something that you hoped for.

Sugar

a sweet white or brown substance that is obtained from plants and used to make food and drinks sweet.

Suitcase

a case for carrying clothes and other items when travelling.

Summer

the warmest season of the year.

Sunflower

a tall plant with large, yellow flowers grown in gardens or for its seeds and their oil that are used in cooking.

Sun

the large bright object in the sky that gives us light and heat, and around which the Earth moves.

Swan

a large bird that is usually white with a long thin neck. Swans live on rivers and lakes.

Sweep

to clean a room, surface, etc. using a broom. Jessica swept the path in front of the house.

Sweet

tasting as if the thing contains a lot of sugar.

Swim

to move thorough water by moving arms and legs.

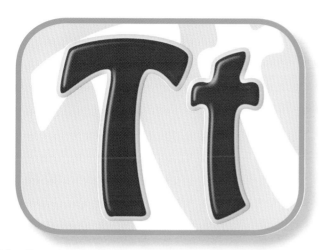

T is the twentieth letter of the English Alphabet.

Table
a piece of furniture with a flat top and legs.

Tail
the part of an animal, bird or fish that sticks out behind the rest of its body.

Tale
a story about things that are made up or imagined. A fairy tale.

Talk
to speak in order to give information or to express feelings.

Tanker
a ship, an aircraft or a road vehicle carrying liquids.

Target
any object aimed at. He threw a dart at the target.

Tall
having of more than average height. John is young and tall.

Taste
the quality of different foods and drinks that is noticed by the tongue.

Tattoo
a mark or design made on the skin by pricking it with needles and filling them with coloured ink.

Taxi
a car with a driver that you pay to take you somewhere.

Teacher
someone who helps you learn in a school or college.

Team
a group of people working together at a particular job.

Teeth

the hard white, bony parts in the mouth used for biting and chewing food. The human adult has 32 teeth.

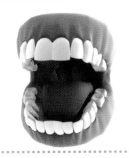

Telephone

an instrument for speaking to someone who is far away.

Television

an electrical machine with a screen on which you can watch programmes with moving pictures and sound.

Tent

a temporary shelter made of canvas or other material.

Textbook

a book that teaches a particular subject.

Thermometer

an instrument for measuring temperature.

Throat

a passage in the neck, leading to stomach and lungs. He has a sore throat.

Thumb

the short, thick finger nearest the wrist. He finally gave the thumbs up to the project.

Ticket

a printed paper slip that allows the certain right, like to travel or to go into a theater, etc.

Tiger

a large, fierce cat that has tan coat with black stripes.
The tiger is a member of the cat family.

Time

a period that has ever been or ever will be. Time is measured in seconds, minutes, hours, days, weeks, months, and years.

Toe

one of the five parts that stick out from the foot.

Tomato

soft, tangy, red or yellow round fruit with juicy pulp.

Tongue

the fleshy muscular organ in the mouth, used in tasting, licking and for speech.

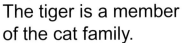

Top
a child's toy that is shaped like a cone. A top spins around on its point when you twist it.

Toy
an object for children to play with. Annie bought toys for the baby.

Tractor
a motor vehicle used for hauling, especially farm machinery, heavy loads, etc.

Train
a railway that has an engine that pulls a number of coaches taking people and goods from one place to another.

Tray
a flat piece of wood, metal or plastic for carrying food or other things.

Tree
a plant with a trunk, leaves, and roots. Birds make their nests on top of the tree.

Triangle
a plane figure with three sides and three angles.

Trousers
a piece of clothing that covers the body from the waist down, covering each leg separately.

Truck
a road vehicle for carrying heavy loads.

T-shirt
a simple shirt without collar or buttons.

Tuition
the act of teaching someone, especially to one person or to people in small group.

Turban
a long piece of cloth wound tightly around the head.

Turtle
a slow-moving reptile with a hard round shell, and flipper-like limbs for swimming.

Twin
two children (brothers and/or sisters) who are born at the same time to the same mother.

Tyre
a rubber covering placed around a wheel. Tyres are hard and black.

abcdefghijklmnopqrstuvwxyz

U is the twenty-first letter of the English Alphabet.

Ugly
very unattractive and unpleasant to look at. An ugly face.

Ukulele
a small musical instrument with four strings.

Umbrella
an object made of cloth or plastic that is stretched over a folding frame and that protects people from the rain.

Under
in a position that is below something. The baby is under the table.

Underpass
a road or path that goes under another road or railway track.

Unfit
not good enough; not in good physical or mental condition. He has been ill and is quite unfit to travel.

Unhappy
not happy; miserable. This girl seems to be unhappy.

Unicorn
a mythical one-horned animal, like a horse with one horn in the centre of its forehead.

Uniform
special clothes worn by members of a group, or by children at school.

Up
towards or in a higher place. The sun comes up at dawn. Timmy pointed and said, she lives just up the street.

Upset
an unhappy and worried mental state. John is upset because his mother did not allow him to go out and play.

V is the twenty-second letter of the English Alphabet.

Vacuum cleaner

a device used to clean floors, rugs, and furniture.

Vampire
an imaginary person who moves about at night to drink blood of sleeping people.

Various
of many different kinds. There are candies available in various flavours.

Vase
a container for flowers. This flower vase looks very beautiful.

Vegetable
plant or part of a plant that is used as food. Green vegetables are good for health.

Vehicle
a thing that is used for transporting people or things from one place to another, such as a car, truck, van, etc.

Victory
success in a game, an election, a contest, a war, etc.

Videogame
a game that is played using some kind of electronic screen.

Violin
a stringed instrument that is played with a bow.

Voice
sound uttered by the mouth. To raise her voice she used microphone.

Volcano
a hill or mountain with an opening through which gases or lava are forced out into the air.

Vulture
a big, bald-headed bird that eats dead animals.

W is the twenty-third letter of the English Alphabet.

Wagon
a railway carriage for carrying heavy loads.

Waiter
a person whose job is to serve customers food and drink at their tables in a restaurant, etc.

Walk
to move along on foot at a normal speed. She walked with her father to get to school.

Walnut
an edible nut with a hard, wrinkled shell.

Walrus
a large sea animal with thick fur and ivory tusks.

Wardrobe
a large cupboard for hanging clothes. Please hang your clothes in the wardrobe.

Washing Machine
a machine for washing clothes, linen, etc. I have bought new washing machine.

Watch
a small clock that you wear on your wrist.

Water
a liquid that is used for washing, drinking, etc.

Wave
a raised line of water that moves along the surface of sea, ocean, etc.

Wedding
a marriage ceremony. They looked very happy on their wedding day.

Week

a period of seven days: Sunday, Monday, Tuesday, Wednesday, Thursday, Friday, and Saturday.

Weigh

to find out how heavy someone or something is by using a scale.

Wet

covered or soaked with some liquid, especially water.

Whale

a very large animal that lives in the sea and looks like a very large fish.

Wheel

one of the round objects under a car, bicycle, bus, etc. that turns when it moves.

Whisper

to speak, or say in a very low, soft voice so that other people cannot hear what you are saying.

Whistle

a metal or plastic instrument that one blows to make a loud high sound. Stop work when the whistle blows.

White

having the colour of fresh snow or of milk.

Wind

air that blows outside as a result of natural forces. Strong winds and heavy rains made the umbrella fly.

Windmill

a tall thin structure with parts that turn round, used to change the power of the wind into electricity.

Window

an opening in the wall or roof of a building, car, etc. usually covered with glass. You can see out a window.

a b c d e f g h i j k l m n o p q r s t u v **w** x y z

W

Wing

one of the parts of a body of a bird, insect or bat that it uses for flying.

Winter

the coldest season of the year between the fall and spring. We wear woollen clothes in winters.

Wire

metal that has been pulled into a thin thread and that is used to carry an electric current or signal.

Witch

a woman who is believed to have magical power, especially to do evil things.

Wolf

a furry large, wild animal that looks like a dog.

Woman

an adult female human being. Shelly is a charming young woman.

Wool

soft, long thread make from the hair of sheep used for knitting.

Work

to do something that involves physical or mental effort, especially as part of a job.

Worksheet

a piece of paper on which there is a series of questions to be done by a student.

Worm

a small, creeping animal with a long, soft body. Worms have no legs and backbone.

Wrist

the joint between the hand and the arm.

Write

to put letters or numbers on paper using a pen or a pencil.

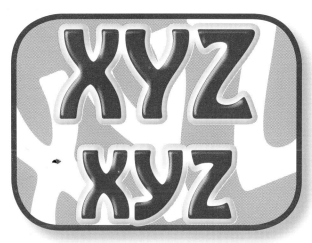

X is the twenty-fourth letter of the English Alphabet.

Xerox
to make a copy of letter, document, etc. by using a Xerox machine.

Xmas
short form of 'Christmas'. We celebrate Xmas on 25 December every year.

X-ray
an image taken by x-rays showing bones or organs in the body.

Xylophone
a musical instrument that has rows of bars and is played with a mallet.

Y is the twenty-fifth letter of the English Alphabet.

Yacht
a large sailing boat that can sail very fast, used for pleasure trips and racing.

Yak
an animal with long hair and long horns.

Yawn
to open the mouth wide and breathe in deeply through it. Sometimes people yawn when they are tired.

Yell
to shout in a very loud voice. Tom yelled out, 'Help me!'

Yellow
having the colour of sunflower.

Yoghurt

a thick white liquid food made from milk. A cup of strawberry yoghurt.

Yolk

the yellow internal part in the centre of an egg.

Yo-Yo

a round toy that consists of two round pieces of wood or plastic joined together, with a piece of string between them. Yo-Yo goes up and down on a string.

Yummy

very good to eat. A yummy pastry.

Z is the twenty-sixth letter of the English Alphabet.

Zebra

an African wild animal that is related to horse. Zebras have black and white stripes.

Zigzag

a line or pattern connected by sharp turns or angles.

Zip

a thing consisting of two rows of metal or plastic teeth that you use to fasten clothes, bags, etc.

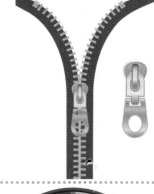

Zodiac

a circular diagram representing the 12 zodiacal signs.

Zoo

a place where many kinds of wild animals are kept for the public to see.

Zoom

to make a distant object appear closer by using a lens.

Zucchini

a type of vegetable with dark green skin and white flesh.